WEDDING BIRDS

D1080699

Wedding Birds

O here's a wed - ding feast of birds! Now
list - en for they sing these words. Fal - de
la - la - la, fal - de la - la - la, fal - de -
la - la - la - la - la.

Now sing the rest of the song!

For Monika Hocke

10 9 8 7 6 5 4 3 2 1

British Library Cataloguing in Publication Data available.

ISBN 0 86264 139 X

This book has been printed on acid-free paper

WEDDING BIRDS

JUTTA ASH

English version by Naomi Lewis

Andersen Press · London

O here's a wedding feast of birds!
Now listen, for they sing these words.

The BLACKBIRD is the handsome groom,
And he will see his bride at noon.

The THRUSH, she is the bride today.
A bunch of may is her bouquet.

The FINCH, the FINCH flies fast to bring
The bride white stockings in her wing.

The COCKATOO, the COCKATOO
He brings the bride her silken shoe.

The CUCKOO flies from nest to nest.
"Cuckoo! I bring the wedding dress!"

The SPARROW's light and swift of wing.
Who else should fetch the wedding ring?

The VULTURE speeds through wind and rain
And safely brings the bridal train.

The HOOPOE comes from far away
To bring, to bring the bridal spray.

The DOVE, who has composed a sonnet,
Sings, then hands the bride her bonnet.

The bright green WOODPECKER, with care
Now combs and curls her shining hair.

The LARK swoops neatly from the birch
In time to take the bride to church.

The MOUNTAINCOCK comes from his rock
All ready in his parson's frock.

The RAVEN wise has worked all night
At dishes for each bird's delight.

The PARROT, with inviting squawk
Gives every bird a knife and fork.

The CRESTED TIT calls, "No mistake!
Though small, I bring the wedding cake."

The NIGHTINGALE now lifts his voice.
"The ball has started! Dance, rejoice!"

The DUCKS arriving from the stream
Together make the music team.

The PEACOCK with a haunting sound
Dances the bride around, around.

The OWL, the mother of the bride,
Has said goodbye, and waved and cried.

The MAGPIE views the clutter-clutter,
Says, "Tut, tut!" and shuts the shutter.

The SNIPE holds up the candle bright
And wishes bride and groom "Goodnight!"

Now you are wed, as man and wife,
As rich or poor, for life, for life.

Hush! The wedding feast is done.
Sing softly, tweet, and caw, and coo.
All birds must rest now in their nest
Till the sun wakes them and you, and you
Till the sun wakes them and you.